CHRIST-CENTERED HIGHER EDUCATION

Why it matters today more than ever

A conversation with:

Dr. Donald W. Sweeting,
president of Colorado Christian University

Dr. Barry Corey,
president of Biola University

Dr. R. Albert Mohler Jr.,
president of The Southern Baptist Theological Seminary

Dr. Philip G. Ryken,
president of Wheaton College

COLORADO CHRISTIAN UNIVERSITY
Grace and Truth

Copyright © 2019, Colorado Christian University

Edited by Kerry Bleikamp, Aaron Burnett, Ian Clary, Christine Franz, and Lance Oversole

Book design by Martha Snowbarger

ISBN: 9781696926997

No part of this publication may be reproduced, distributed, translated, stored in a retrieval system, or transmitted in any form or by any means, including electronic, mechanical, photocopying, microphone, recording, or otherwise, without written permission from Colorado Christian University.

Printed in the United States of America

Contents

Preface	iv
Introduction	1
Three Distinguished Christian Educators	3
Jesus and the University	5
Why Does the Christian Faith Inspire Learning?	11
The Advantages of a Christian Liberal Arts Education	15
Contemporary Educational Disorder: All is Not Well in Our Universities	18
Staying Faithful as a Christian College	23
Advice for Students and Prospective Students	27
A Final Word	29
Notes	33
Additional Resources	34

Preface

Every week seems to bring a new story about the deteriorating state of American higher education.

Our universities not only lack a unifying center, but they seem disoriented. They appear to be descending into a moral, spiritual, and intellectual chaos that is undermining the entire educational enterprise. There is a skepticism about truth, virtue, meaning, and reason. There is a growing hostility toward the entire Western tradition upon which the university was built. That's why I want you to think for a few minutes about a special kind of university—a Christian university—not Christian in name only, but one that is convictionally Christian. I want you to consider why it is unique and why it is needed now more than ever.

I invite you to listen in on a very important conversation about higher education that took place between four leaders in Christian higher education: Philip Ryken, president of Wheaton College; Albert Mohler, president of The Southern Baptist Theological Seminary and Boyce College; Barry Corey, president of Biola University; and me.

It was my honor to host this conversation as a prelude to my inauguration at Colorado Christian University. The conversation was about a topic that has only grown more timely due to the events unfolding before our eyes. The topic was "Christ-centered higher education: why it matters today more than ever."

Listening in to this conversation will be a great benefit for students, faculty, staff, trustees, prospective students, parents of students, and all who are interested in the work of a Christian college or university. In it I asked my distinguished guests to help us make connections that perhaps you have not made before. I wanted them to help answer questions such as:

- What is so special about a Christian college or university?
- What does Jesus Christ have to do with the university?
- What is the deep connection between faith and learning?
- How is a Christian education unique?
- Why is the Western university in a state of crisis?
- What are the advantages of a Christian liberal arts education, and how can we preserve the uniqueness of this kind of education?
- Finally, how can students get the most out of this kind of education?

That's a tall order for a short forum. But my guests are outstanding Christian educators who lead venerable institutions; I want us to hear what they have to say.

To get the kind of wisdom they offer here, one often has to wade through several thick volumes, each dealing with any one of the questions I have posed. The uniqueness of this discussion is that my friends quickly get to the point and concisely lay out important answers that all of us need to hear.

Why do we need to hear these answers? So that we know how special the endeavor is in which we are involved.

If you are an educational leader, you need to hear this so that you do everything you can to preserve Christian higher education and help it to flourish in the days ahead—days when the wider society, and sometimes even our government, question our mission, or actually seek to undermine it.

If you are a student, you need to hear this so that you will realize the unique privilege you have in studying at a Christian university.

If you are a parent or donor, you need to hear this so that you will do everything you can to help these institutions flourish.

In His service,
Donald W. Sweeting, Ph.D.
President, Colorado Christian University

CHRIST-CENTERED HIGHER EDUCATION

Why it matters today more than ever

*"There are few
earthly things
more splendid
than a university."*

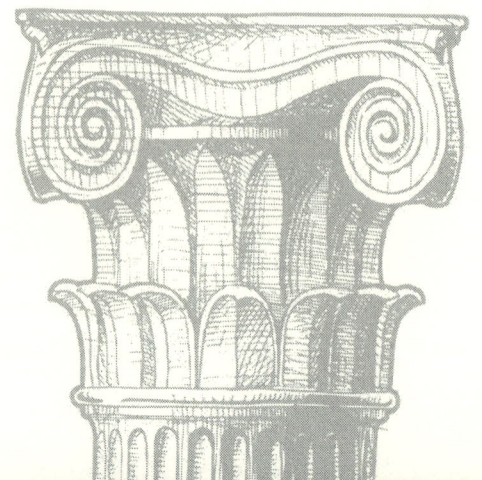

INTRODUCTION

Dr. Sweeting:
In the aftermath of World War II, on June 25, 1946, Britain's poet laureate, John Masefield (1930–1967), was asked to write a poem for the inauguration of the chancellor of the University of Sheffield. It was entitled: "A University: Splendid, Beautiful and Enduring." Here are some of his words:

> ... *There are few earthly things more splendid than a university.*
> *In these days of broken frontiers and collapsing values,*
> *when the dams are down and the floods are making misery,*
> *when every ancient foothold has become something of a quagmire,*
> *wherever a university stands, it stands and shines;*
> *wherever it exists, the free minds of men,*
> *urged on to full and fair enquiry,*
> *may still bring wisdom into human affairs.*
> *There are few earthly things more beautiful than a university.*
> *It is a place where those who hate ignorance may strive to know,*
> *where those who perceive truth may strive to make others see;*
> *where seekers and learners alike,*
> *banded together in the search for knowledge,*
> *will honour thought in all its finer ways,*
> *will welcome thinkers in distress or in exile,*
> *will uphold ever the dignity of thought and learning*
> *and will exact standards in these things.*

Immediately after the war, Masefield was captivated by the glory and possibilities of a university. The university was a beacon of light, a place to search after truth, to grow in wisdom, and a place of open inquiry and respect. In his mind, there was nothing so splendid, beautiful, and enduring.

Fast forward 70 years and things are not so splendid. Our universities are committedly "post"—post-truth (outside of the sciences, the existence of objective truth is largely denied), post-virtue (moral relativism is widely taught and embraced), post-meaning (the question of life's meaning is not addressed), not to mention post-Christian. There is hostility toward great books, great ideas, and great lives since such a tradition is said to be elitist, rooted in the intellectual and artistic achievements of the West.

We hear about the coddling of students—trigger warnings and safe spaces to protect students from ideas or opinions they may find objectionable. Dissenting speakers are sometimes disinvited or shouted down. We've read news stories about the mobs at Middlebury, Claremont McKenna College, and UC Berkeley. The *Chronicle of Higher Education* recently reported that intimidation is the new normal on college campuses, stating, "From now on, any speaker who arouses a protest is at risk of a beating."[1]

Collegiality is disappearing from too many colleges. Rational argument and freedom of thought, like freedom of religion, are in retreat. A new illiberal liberalism is descending on the academy.

Meanwhile, alumni of many of our universities are realizing that their *alma mater* is not what she used to be. Prospective students and their parents also sense something is deeply wrong. Perhaps this is one reason why many Americans appear to be losing faith in the value of a college education. They often ask: "Why spend a great deal of money to invest in an education like that?"

This is what makes our topic so timely. It is my belief that Christ-centered higher education matters today more than ever. It is an extraordinary time to be a president at a Christian university. The opportunities to train up a new generation of students are immense. But the craziness seen on campuses across the country is stunning.

THREE DISTINGUISHED CHRISTIAN EDUCATORS

Dr. Sweeting:
It is a joy to have with us today some very special friends and leaders in Christian higher education. I want you to hear from them as we think about this important issue. Let me introduce them in a little more detail.

Our first guest is Dr. Barry Corey, president of Biola University. Barry earned his Ph.D. from Boston College and completed his Bachelor of Arts in English and Biblical Studies at Evangel University. He is a Fulbright Scholar and vice-chair of the board of directors for the Council of Christian Colleges and Universities. He helped lead the response to California Bill 1146 that threatened many Christian universities, and we're so grateful to Barry for his leadership in that initiative.

Our next guest is Dr. Phil Ryken, the eighth president of Wheaton College. Phil earned his doctorate from Oxford University and his Master of Divinity from Westminster Theological Seminary. He graduated from Wheaton College, where his dad was also a professor. For 15 years, he was the pastor of Tenth Presbyterian Church in Philadelphia. He's written over 40 books and is a board member of the Council for Christian Colleges and Universities. We are blessed to have Dr. Ryken join us today.

Also with us is Dr. Albert Mohler. He is the president of The Southern Baptist Theological Seminary, one of the largest seminaries in the world, and is also president of Boyce College. He's a theologian. He served as pastor in several Southern Baptist churches, went to Samford University, and earned his Doctor in Philosophy and M.Div. from Southern Seminary. He serves as a professor of Christian Theology at Southern. He's written numerous books, most recently, *The Conviction to Lead*, and

We Cannot be Silent. In addition to his presidential duties, he has two podcasts that are heard by many, many people. One is called "The Briefing," a daily analysis of Christian news and events from a Christian worldview, and "Thinking in Public," a series of conversations with today's leading thinkers. He's a leader in the Southern Baptist Convention and has served on numerous boards.

Each of our guests are extraordinary Christian leaders. They love students and are passionate advocates for the cause of Christ-centered higher learning.

JESUS AND THE UNIVERSITY

Dr. Sweeting:
With this in mind, let me start our conversation by asking the question: What does Jesus Christ have to do with the founding of the Western university?

Dr. Ryken:
First of all, let me just say it's a huge privilege for us to be here with Don Sweeting. This is a man of substance. You're going to like him better and better, even more than you do now. I think it's so appropriate for us to be talking about this question because an inauguration like this is really not about celebrating a person or even celebrating an institution. While this is an amazing opportunity to celebrate Colorado Christian University, it's really about celebrating the whole kingdom enterprise of Christian education, how important it is, and how important it is in God's purposes.

I would like to go back to the founding of Harvard University. The founders of Harvard, at the beginning of higher education in the United States, said, "We want to lay Jesus Christ at the bottom, as the foundation of everything we're going to do in this college."

Jesus Christ has everything to do with the founding of universities in the United States, but there's a longer tradition—even going back to the early centuries of the church. That's absolutely the starting point.

Dr. Mohler:
I would simply say that if we take seriously the New Testament witness of Christ as the *Alpha* and the *Omega*, the Beginning and the End, if we believe that He is preeminent over all things, then we

"Jesus Christ has everything to do with the founding of universities in the United States, but there's a longer tradition—even going back to the early centuries of the church."

understand that He stands in judgment over and as the sole explanation of the existence of all things. That would include even the most massive secular modern research university that thinks of itself as having no accountability to Christ and traces its origins to Christ in no way.

The role of the modern university is inseparable from the Christian church. It was love of learning based upon love of God and loving your neighbor that drove the development of the modern university. It was the understanding of the universals and the unity of truth—not the unity of truth in truth, but the unity of truth in Christ. It was that deep Christian impulse that led to the development of the university.

You look at these massively influential, prestigious, and in many ways, wonderful intuitions of higher education. Most of the students, faculty, and trustees have no idea how they arrived at this. In many ways, they've lost the vision of what a university wants to be. They're actually taking apart the universals that the university itself was established to represent.

I'm so thankful today for this event, for your new president, and for all the Christian institutions of higher education represented here today, because this is the recovery effort—back to the origins of the university in Christian learning and love of Christ.

Dr. Corey:

I am honored to be here today, President Sweeting. I can tell the students love you here, as they should. You're going to make such a difference, you and your wife, Christina, as well. It's wonderful to see you, your wife, and your family here.

Students, when I was your age, I actually read an essay called "The Idea of University," written by Cardinal John Henry Newman. That's one of the reasons why I'm in higher education from a faith tradition today, because it was so impactful for me to see the cohesiveness of how the university was supposed to be. As Dr. Mohler said, the "uni" in university has been lost. It was Clark Kerr, the guru of higher education at California State University, who said it's really a "multiversity" because it's been so scattered. We [Christian universities] actually keep the "uni" in university.

Also, there's been this institutional drift that was alluded to. We're not asking how do we take those universities that once were deeply rooted in the centrality of Christ and formation of being rooted in God's Word and bring them back. Instead, we're asking how do we make sure that we stay faithful? That's the question for us.

There is an interesting story about Emerson Hall at Harvard, named after the Unitarian minister Ralph Waldo Emerson. The hall was dedicated just last century. Everyone thought that when they unveiled the saying on the top of the building, it was going to be, "Man is the measure of all things," since Emerson Hall houses the philosophy department. Instead, when it was unveiled it said, "What is man that thou art mindful of Him? Psalm 8:4." I think even in these universities, there's something transcendent that leads to the centrality of Christ, but is not recognized, is not acknowledged, but we're recovering it, we're maintaining it, we're preserving it.

Dr. Ryken:

Don, one of my hopes for an event like this is that students would remember this and realize that they have a long-term vested interest in the flourishing of Christian colleges and universities. Many of you are going to have opportunities to serve in other colleges and universities, to support them financially and in other ways. Those of us who are involved in Christian higher education are a little bit haunted by the ghosts of Christianity on the campuses of many of the great colleges and universities of this country—schools that are now thoroughly secular.

Here's another story. One of our faculty members was on the campus of a well-known, highly ranked university in the United States and noticed in the ground, the original university motto. The motto spoke about the love of learning for the sake of God. It brought together the life of the mind and the life of submission to God. As she was reading these gothic letters out loud to her family, a faculty member from that institution came up and wanted to engage in conversation because that faculty member was a Christian. Our faculty member mentioned that she taught at Wheaton College. This faculty member from this other university said, "You're fortunate because you still have that mission and we don't."

Part of why we need to be committed to one another and really committed to Christ is that we would sustain the life of learning in submission to Christ from one generation to the next. That's why this is an important landmark occasion.

"God made us
in His image.
The *imago dei* means
many things, but at the
very least it means
we're cognitive beings.
He made us beings
who want to know."

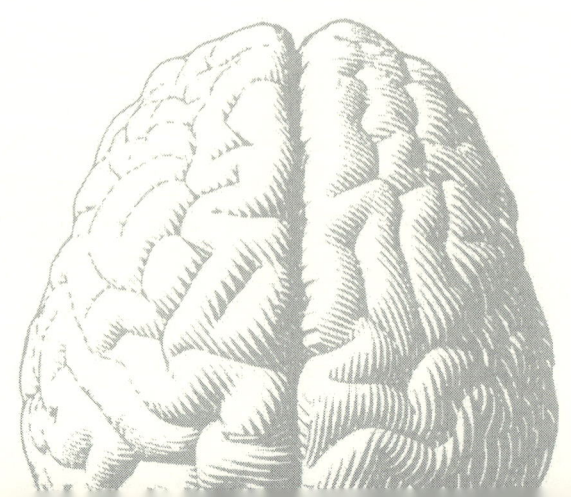

WHY DOES THE CHRISTIAN FAITH INSPIRE LEARNING?

Dr. Sweeting:

What is it about the Christian faith and knowing Christ that sparks this drive to learn and educate? When we look at the history of the early church, we discover that when missionaries were sent out and found people groups that did not have a written language, they would actually invent one so that a tribe or society could read the Bible. It appears that anywhere the gospel went, literacy followed, and then schools of higher learning. So what is it that makes this happen?

Dr. Mohler:

Well, I'll just go to theology. God made us in His image. The *imago dei* means many things, but at the very least it means we're cognitive beings. He made us beings who want to know. We want to understand. We want to be able to describe. We are natural teachers and we're naturally taught. Then I go to Genesis 1:28,[2] that dominion mandate, which certainly includes learning. You can't possibly fulfill what God has assigned us in Genesis 1:28, without learning.

Look at how in the Old Testament people of God honored learning. Look at how often the central command given to parents was to teach. Look at how honored Solomon is for asking for wisdom. By the time you get to the New Testament, you not only have the Christian inheritance of the synagogue and Jewish models of education, but you have early Christians taking the very best of Greek and Roman models of schools and putting those models together to use them for Christian truth.

You look at a great church father like Augustine who understood the importance of schools. These catechetical schools were schools for new believers. Augustine called them "the incubation chambers of the church." I think that's what makes us so happy here. That's what a Christian college and university really is. The Christian college and university don't have a monopoly on this. That's what every church should be. That's what every Christian home should be. The Christian college and university have a massive role to play in educating us to the glory of God.

Dr. Ryken:

In the early church and in cities like Alexandria and Antioch, Christian people looked at the best of liberal arts education and they said, "If we brought this under the lordship of Jesus Christ, we'd have something of enduring value to teach the young people in our community."

Part of the value in Christian education is the apologetic value. You want to understand the values and ideas of a culture so you can respond to them, engage them, critique them as appropriate, redeem them, and bring them under the lordship of Jesus Christ. Whether it's Alcuin[3] in the courts of Charlemagne advocating for Christ-centered education, or the kind of things you see from Martin Luther and John Calvin about the value of liberal arts learning for Christian young people—Christian education is something that's been a part of the church's inheritance throughout the centuries.

Dr. Corey:

Students, you have an incredible gift to be able to study here at Colorado Christian University. These are some of the most formative years of your life; you're going to be shaped not only intellectually, relationally, and spiritually, but you're going to work on putting that all together. As was said by Abraham Kuyper, "There is no square inch of all creation that Jesus doesn't declare, 'That's mine.'" I think that's exciting and exhilarating for us to think about.

I was in a hotel lobby about a year ago, having a cup of coffee with David Brooks from *The New York Times*. I remember him saying,

"Christian colleges have what everybody else is desperate to have: a way of talking about and educating the human person in a way that integrates faith, emotion, and intellect. You have a recipe to nurture human beings with a dedicated heart, a courageous mind, and a purposeful soul, and almost no other set of institutions in American society has that, and everybody wants it."

Paul says, "Take every opportunity to articulate the reason for what you believe," but do that with gentleness and respect. Maybe that's a word of encouragement to you students who have that deep sense of what you believe—for you to remember to lead with grace, wisdom, kindness, and love. Do that, and it's going to have a remarkable impact on this world.

Dr. Sweeting:

As a pastor, I've seen many people who at first didn't really care about education, but then they embraced the gospel. Once they came to know Christ, the Living Word, all of a sudden, they had a desire to learn more about Him. They wanted to know God's book. So, they suddenly had a whole new motivation to read and learn. Soon they wanted to send their kids to good schools so they would learn even more. There is something about knowing the Living Word, Jesus Christ, that makes people care about words and learning.

Dr. Ryken:

The more deeply we understand that Jesus Christ Himself is the Creator God, then the more we'll understand why everything in the world that He has made is going to be fascinating to us. As a student, when you have that "wow" moment, or when you're able to connect one idea to another idea that really helps you understand what makes human beings tick, or when you're reading great literature and you come to a deeper understanding of something about yourself and who you are, I encourage you go a step deeper and realize this is the way things are because of who Jesus is and the way that He has made things. That immediately leads us to a sense of worship.

"Christian liberal arts education has an integrating coherence because Christ is at the center. It aims to educate the whole person—mind, heart, and will."

THE ADVANTAGES OF A CHRISTIAN LIBERAL ARTS EDUCATION

Dr. Sweeting:
Talk to us about the advantages of a Christian liberal arts education.

Dr. Mohler:
I would start with the immediate. Who in the world, other than those of us gathering in a room like this in similar institutions, would have a conversation like this one? Just to think about the possibility of being in a learning community with others who love Christ, who want to honor Christ, who want to know the world that God has made, and who want to be good stewards of the mind. These are people who also want to be good Christian citizens, neighbors, and want to be faithful teachers and pastors. These are the people who will want to take the gospel to the ends of the earth and will want to know what they need to know to be ready to do just that.

When people my age speak to college students, you have no idea how envious we are of you. Most of us look back to that four-year period of our undergraduate education and understand those as the prized years of our lives. Those are the years that we look back to and say, "There was nothing quite as exhilarating and wonderful as those four years." We're envious in that sense.

I'm also envious of you in another sense. You have even greater opportunities than those who came before you. There are resources for Christian scholarship and there is a community of Christian learning that didn't really exist before. Part of it is because it was forged under diversity. You're looking at the fact that Christian higher education now has to understand itself as not only related to the larger world of higher education, but also distinct from it. Now we see so many secular institutions that were once Christian and we look at so many Christian institutions that have lost their commitment to Christ. I honestly believe there may well be more faithful Christian colleges today on the front lines of scholarship than 50 or 75 years ago.

There's good news. There's plenty to be concerned about, but there's very good news. When I see the activity on a campus like this, and with a new president, I start to look at the plans, not only that the leadership of the school has, but the plans that I believe God has for you. I can only say that a generation later, if the Lord allows, there will be students who will have even greater opportunities than you have. Let's be good stewards of our moment, your moment.

Dr. Ryken:

When we talk about liberal arts learning, we're talking about a comprehensive education that introduces students to the natural world, through the sciences, through the social sciences, through literature, philosophy, music, the arts, and more. I can give you all kinds of reasons why that's a great education. I think research is showing that a liberal arts education is a great education for the working world because most people, as they enter into the working world, aren't going to do one job for 50 years then retire. Students, you're going to have a variety of transitions. You're going to need communication skills, intellectual skills, writing skills, and the critical thinking skills that liberal arts learning cultivates.

Engage in Christian liberal arts learning because it will enable you to do well in your vocation. But do it for the love of learning itself. Have your mind awaken to what God has put into the world and into the human race. Lean into that and find enjoyment in that. For me, that would be reason enough to pursue liberal arts learning.

Dr. Sweeting:

I read an article by Paul J. Maurer, president of Montreat College, and he made an astounding claim. He said, "Christian liberal arts education remains the best education available to humanity."[4]

When I first read that, I thought it might be an exaggeration. But then I got to thinking about it, and I think he is right. Why is it the best kind of education? There are many reasons. It begins with the fear of the Lord, which is the beginning of wisdom. It is open to God's revelation. It is locked into Christ—in whom, as Colossians tells us, are hidden all the treasures of wisdom and knowledge [Col. 2:3]. Christian liberal arts education has an integrating coherence because Christ is at the center. It aims to educate the whole person—mind, heart, and will. It addresses the question of meaning and virtue. It lays the basis for truth and reason. It points to the source of beauty. In sum, it lays out a better vision of what it means to be human.

CONTEMPORARY EDUCATIONAL DISORDER: ALL IS NOT WELL IN OUR UNIVERSITIES

Dr. Sweeting:
We've mentioned some of the signs of the educational disarray in our wider culture. Can you help give us a better sense of what's going on in the wider university world? As I said, all is not well. There is a growing disorientation—help us understand this.

Dr. Corey:
Maybe one way is looking at the critiques of some of the leading universities from within themselves. In Allan Bloom's book, *The Closing of the American Mind*, he said that there is a disconnect in higher education between the intellectual life and the moral life. Anthony Kronman who wrote *Education's End*, said, "Somehow along the way, our universities, our major thought centers, have stopped asking the big questions of life because we've become too segmented, too fragmented, too specialized."

Then, of course, you have Harry Lewis who was the dean at Harvard. He wrote *Education Without a Soul*. In his book, he said that universities have lost their sense of how to fit their problems into an encompassing educational mission, which results in a curriculum with no meaning at all. He asked, "What does the ideal Harvard graduate look like?" In reply he said, "There's no consensus there."

In the Christian university, we have consensus. We have consensus around the lordship of Christ and we have consensus around the authority of God's Word.

My former boss, Walt Kaiser—who was the president of Gordon-Conwell Theological Seminary and a great Old Testament scholar—refers to Proverbs 29:18 which states, "Where there is no vision, people perish." He said, "That literally means where there is no revelatory input of God's Word, people come undone, people come unrestrained." The opposite is true for us, where there is that revelatory input. It holds us together. It is the life of flourishing to which God has called us. It is the created order. It is so rich and so healthy and so life-giving, that we have a very good thing. That is the antidote to the disarray that you were talking about, President Sweeting.

Dr. Ryken:
Also, on many campuses in the United States, there is the pursuit of sinful behavior in an unrestrained way. Whether it's sexual license, profanity, the abuse of drugs and alcohol, what happens particularly to women in so many of our college and university campuses, it's out there.

I'd like to say something about Wheaton that I think you could say about Colorado Christian University. There's no campus in the world that needs the grace of Jesus Christ more than our campus. There's plenty of need for God's grace on our campus in response to sin.

Even having said that, there's something very different about a campus community that says we want to pursue a life of moral integrity, of sexual purity, of wholesome relationships, and even if we fail at that sometimes, we want to confess that and move forward. That's very different from what's happening in a lot of colleges and college dormitories. That's not the only reason to pursue a Christ-centered college education, but it's an important one.

Dr. Mohler:
The biographies of some of the great colleges and universities around us are really interesting and instructive.

I think one of the most interesting places to watch right now is the University of California, Berkeley. It was established by the State of

California to be the great academic institution on the West Coast. It's where the free speech movement emerged in the 1960s and the 1970s, but free speech is basically being shut down on that campus. There was a generation of radicals in the 1960s who are now the tenured professors of the current generation. These professors are being shut down by the students who were on their campus in the year 2017 and the faculty have no idea how to respond to this whatsoever. They have no worldview that would enable them to even offer a cogent argument.

Then there's something else going on at Berkeley that's interesting to watch. The people there are beginning to ask some basic questions about whether they actually are a university. They have people in the sciences who never have contact with those in the humanities because they have completely separate faculty meetings.

One of the professors in the sciences at Berkeley said, "We have no controversy over here. We've got laboratories. You humanities, liberal arts people, you can have all these arguments and protests, not so much here." Well, that's not exactly true. But what is true is that in a Christian understanding, a Christian biblical worldview, nothing is actually separate from anything else. You can't have this balkanization of the disciplines and the guilds. Every class, every faculty member, every department, has to be part of a larger whole, accountable under the lordship of Christ. That's what I think might affect the Christian college and university right now. I think that anyone who walks into a Christian classroom might find that a Christian education is the most refreshing alternative to what's going on in the chaos of higher education today.

Dr. Corey:

To Dr. Mohler's point, it's almost becoming absurd in some universities how they're becoming echo chambers that feed the beast of the university's own ideas. Nicholas Kristof from *The New York Times* just a few weeks ago said, "The lack of ideological diversity on campuses is a disservice to the students and to liberalism itself. With liberalism collapsing on some campuses into self-parody, we liberals champion tolerance—except for conservative and evangelical

Christians. We want to be inclusive to people who don't look like us as long as they think like us."

Dr. Ryken:
I think it's also very important that we're not only reading Christian thinkers, but are broadly exposed to the thinking of the culture. We need to learn what we can from the culture because we could become our own echo chamber if we aren't engaging in the culture that surrounds us.

"Institutions don't drift toward Christ-centeredness, they drift away from it."

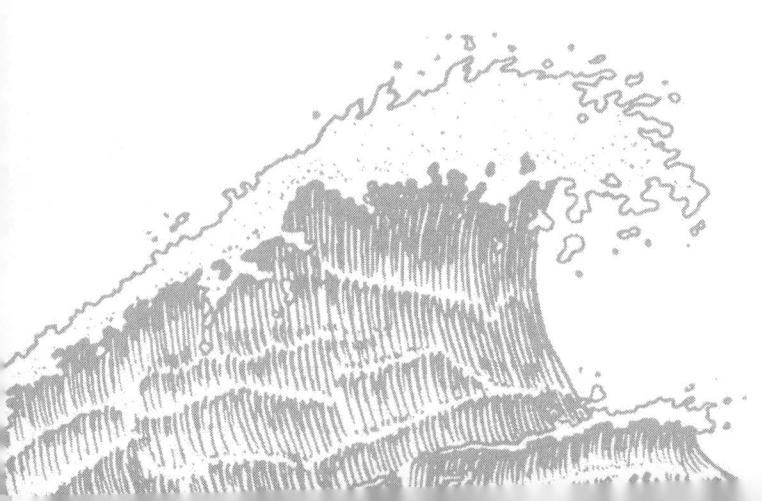

STAYING FAITHFUL
AS A CHRISTIAN COLLEGE

Dr. Sweeting:
At CCU, we aspire to be a Christ-centered university. I know all of you have the same aspiration for your schools. However, looking back at the last 100 years in American history, there's this massive defection. Many institutions that were founded as Christian schools are no longer Christian. In some cases, they teach the exact opposite. How can we stay a Christ-centered institution?

Dr. Corey:
Institutions don't drift toward Christ-centeredness, they drift away from it. Board members who are here, you're not only called to keep your institution physically solvent, but missionally faithful. That happens by the board, by the office of the president, and by the faculty. The three of those constituents, especially, need to work together to reclaim with every generation that this is a profoundly Christ-centered university, and that means God's Word matters. That means that spiritual formation isn't just about what we understand intellectually, but also how we live out our faith and how we do so in a way that is of profound gospel service to our community.

If board meetings aren't regularly talking about what it means to be missionally faithful, and are instead only talking about what it means to be fiscally solvent, then there needs to be a recalibration.

Dr. Ryken:
It's only with great prayer and difficulty that an institution remains faithful to Christ. I think you see that in Scripture. It was hard for the

people of God in the Old Testament to remain faithful from generation to generation. We can also see how difficult it was for the early Christian church to find unity. It's always a huge challenge to us.

I'll say in addition to the trustees that are here for this inauguration, there are also probably some future trustees, so it's good for all of us to be thinking about what it is going to take for a school like this one to become more Christ-centered.

I'll just highlight one thing that's super important, and that's hiring. The staff that you hire, the faculty that you hire, the new trustees that you invite, you need to ask what is their theological commitment, what is their spiritual life, and then remain accountable to one another. The same kind of drifting away from Christ that can happen to an institution can also happen to individuals.

The institutions that will remain faithful over the long term are not ones where you don't have any controversy. They are ones that from time to time will have controversy, because that's part of the cost of remaining faithful.

Dr. Mohler:

I do not think there is any hope for an institution of Christian higher education that is not rightly bound, confessionally, to the articulation of the Christian faith. That binding is not merely symbolic, but it is also covenantal. It is what is expected of everyone. That means that no one should be invited to serve on the board of trustees if they do not willingly and eagerly affirm belief in that confessional statement.

In terms of hiring and in terms of the messaging of the institution, these must be very clear because they state who you are. But that's not enough. To the Board of Trustees, I want to say that you, by law and by fiduciary responsibility, are the governing board of this institution. You, above all, in the beginning and in the end, will be responsible for whether or not this university remains distinctively and faithfully Christian.

One of the ways you must do that is to make sure that you talk about this and take nothing for granted. I think one of the things you have to watch out for in board meetings is if you're only talking about matters that are pragmatic and strategic, such as financials. If you're not talking about the spiritual substance and life of this college, that shows your priorities for the institution. Inevitably, there will not only be drift, there will be a disaster.

The most important action a governing board takes is the election of a chief executive officer. It is the board's responsibility to empower that president to do the job that is assigned. Thus, the president must be fully authorized and responsible when it comes to hiring. The board must not only be aware of that, but knowledgeable about that and take ownership of it as well.

Again, when hiring faculty, you shouldn't be looking for faculty that can sign your doctoral statement. You need to be looking for faculty who can't wait to teach in an institution that believes as you believe in terms of theology, morality, worldview, and your education mission.

There are a couple of other breaking points; one of them is finances. James Tunstead's book, *Dying of the Light*, chronicles the loss of educational institutions. He shows that many of these schools were lost during the Great Depression when the churches were no longer able to support them financially. They had to be supported by wealthy laypersons who said, "We'll support them financially, but we will then control them."

Let me state this, I hope that this is a wealthy, well-endowed, wonderfully resourced Christian university. I hope all the dreams on the wall become true and more, but it would be better to be poor and faithful, than rich and unfaithful. Just keep that in mind.

One last trip wire is in enrollment. People should know that this is a Christian university. There should be no allowance for accommodation just for the cause of having a larger enrollment. That's just another way of getting to the same disaster.

"… study what you love. … You might be thinking of studying something that's useful, but God has given you passions for a reason."

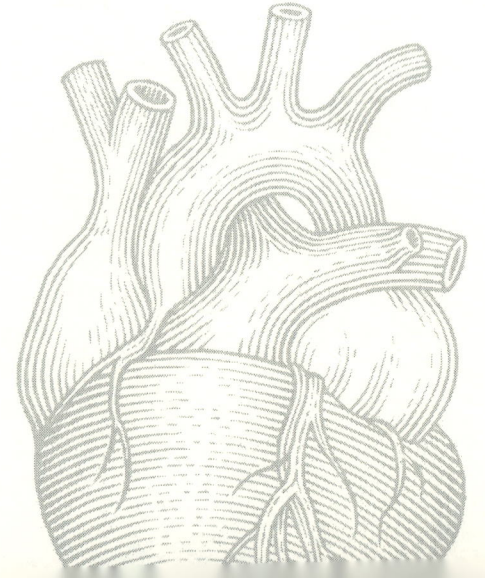

ADVICE FOR STUDENTS AND PROSPECTIVE STUDENTS

Dr. Sweeting:
As we get ready to close, I want to ask you one last question. Many students are listening to this conversation. What advice do you have for students? What would you say to them?

Dr. Ryken:
I can keep it very simple. I would say these two things; number one, more Jesus. More Jesus in your life. More of the Word of God. More worship. More conversation about spiritual things. You will be greatly blessed the more of Jesus that you have in your life in every way.

The other thing I say is study what you love. Your parents might have a slightly different idea than that. You might be thinking of studying something that's useful, but God has given you passions for a reason. He will use them in your long-term calling. I'm not opposed to adding a second major that you think will make you more marketable. I also definitely agree in doing internships and being strategic about how you use your summers for professional preparation. But ultimately, study what you love.

Dr. Corey:
What I've been telling students at Biola recently is to live a life with a firm center and soft edges. That firm center is made up of our deep, core convictions. This is what I believe, and a lot of that is nurtured on your knees. Cultivating your relationship with Christ through studying His Word, through meditating on it, and through the relationships that you have, will allow that core to be strengthened. In this world we need

Christians that lead with a great sense of kindness and wisdom. Kindness, I've been saying recently, is not a random act. It's a radical life that Jesus has called you to and you live that out, even though sometimes you might be rejected. Sometimes you'll be accepted, but you'll never be forgotten when you live that way. Our world needs this next generation to spread the aroma of Christ and smell like Jesus wherever they go.

Dr. Mohler:

There are a couple of things I encourage our students about; one of them is that the opportunity for residential higher education is very rare. Don't waste the opportunity. People are going to come to this campus and speak. You'll be tempted to do something else, but I encourage you to go hear them speak. You're never going to see them again. You have no idea what might make an impact on your life that you weren't planning.

The other thing I'd like to mention is friendship. You thought the friends you made in high school were going to last a lifetime. By now, you've figured out they didn't. But you're in a completely different situation now, and I will tell you, many of the friends you make here will be friends for a lifetime. Lean into them, love them, and get ready to live life together.

The third thing I'm going to encourage you to do is be deeply involved in the life of a local church. It's very tempting while you are in college to think that college is my church. It's not. You need to be deeply involved in the life of a local church. You'll be spiritually healthier. You also need to be in a place where there are little people and old people who you love and can worship alongside.

A FINAL WORD

Dr. Sweeting:
With that, I'm afraid we have to bring our conversation to an end.

I think that we've answered the question that we've asked, "Does Christ-centered university education matter today, more than ever?" The answer is a resounding, "Yes!" It matters historically. It matters intellectually. It matters spiritually. It matters because the biggest issue in higher education today is the center. Is there a center? Yes, there is. The Apostle Paul gets right to the point in Colossians 1:17 when he says, "He (that is, Jesus) is before all things, and in Him all things hold together."

We've been so blessed to have our three guests here with us today. Thank you Dr. Mohler, Dr. Ryken, and Dr. Corey for being with us. Thank you for helping us see that a Christ-centered university education still matters, in fact, I think we would all say, that it matters more than ever.

This is important for each of us to grasp. It is important for students, that you know the immense privilege you have when you study at a school that strives to be both a university and convictionally Christian. It is important for faculty to realize the important role you have in shaping a new generation of students. It is important for staff to see that for which you are ultimately working. It is important for alumni to see that our colleges and universities need your continued support. It is important for pastors and Christian leaders. All of us here today want to see our schools serve and bless the church. And it is important for trustees—you are stewards over these important institutions—to see that they remain healthy and faithful. You will have to answer to the Lord for what happened on your watch.

"… we have a responsibility to provide an education that is characterized by academic excellence and academic faithfulness."

Each of us presidents realize that we have a responsibility to provide an education that is characterized by academic excellence and academic faithfulness. The challenges we face in leading these schools are considerable. We would ask you to pray for us, and for the sake of the kingdom, help us flourish. We ask that when those times come, as they surely will, when opposition arises to the very mission of our schools, please speak up for us, and be a voice for our first freedom—religious freedom—so that we can continue the important work that God has called us to.

Notes

1. Haidt, Jonathan, "Intimidation Is the New Normal on Campus," *The Chronicle of Higher Education*, (April 26, 2017).

2. "And God blessed them. And God said to them, 'Be fruitful and multiply and fill the earth and subdue it, and have dominion over the fish of the sea and over the birds of the heavens and over every living thing that moves on the earth,'" (Genesis 1:28, ESV).

3. Alcuin of York (*ca.* 740–804) was responsible for educational reforms during the Carolingian Renaissance.

4. Maurer, Paul J., "The Enduring Value of a Christian Liberal Arts Education," *Christian Research Journal*, (Volume 38, Number 04, 2015).

Additional Resources

Black, Jim Nelson, *Freefall of the American University: How Our Colleges Are Corrupting the Minds and Morals of the Next Generation*, WND Books, 2004.

Bloom, Allan, *The Closing of the American Mind, How Higher Education Has Failed Democracy and Impoverished the Souls of Today's Students*, Simon and Schuster, 2012, first published 1987.

Buckley, William F., *God and Man at Yale*, Henry Regnery, 1951.

Burtchaell, James Tunstead, *The Dying of the Light: The Disengagement of Colleges and Universities from their Christian Churches*, Eerdmans, 1998.

Fant, Gene C., *The Liberal Arts: A Student's Guide*, Crossway, 2012.

Dockery, Davis S. and Timothy George, *The Great Tradition of Christian Thinking: A Student's Guide*, Crossway, 2012.

Furedi, Frank, *What's Happened to the University? A Sociological Exploration of Its Infantilization*, Routledge, 2017.

Glanzer, Perry L., Allenman, Nathan F., Ream, Todd C., *Restoring the Soul of the University: Unifying Christian Higher Education in a Fragmented Age*, IVP Academic, 2017.

Holmes, Kim, *The Closing of the Liberal Mind, How Groupthink and Intolerance Define the Left*, Encounter Books, 2016.

Holmes, Arthur, *The Idea of a Christian College*, Eerdmans, 1975.

Kirk, Russell, *Decadence and Renewal in the Higher Learning*, Gateway Editions, 1978.

Kronman, Anthony T., *Education's End: Why Our Colleges and Universities Have Given Up on the Meaning of Life*, Yale University Press, 2007.

Malik, Charles Habib, *A Christian Critique of the University*, InterVarsity Press, 1982.

Marsden, George M., *The Outrageous Idea of Christian Scholarship*, Oxford University Press, 1997.

Marsden, George M., *The Soul of the American University: From Protestant Establishment to Established Nonbelief*, Oxford University Press, 1994.

Newman, John Henry, *The Idea of a University*, UBI Caritas Press, 2015, first published in 1852.

Left to right: Dr. Philip G. Ryken, Dr. Donald W. Sweeting, Dr. Barry Corey, and Dr. R. Albert Mohler Jr.

Made in the USA
Columbia, SC
19 August 2021

44004942R00029